Reading Level
4. 1

AR Points
0.5

56624

9667

by Victor Gentle and Janet Perry

Gareth Stevens Publishing
A WORLD ALMANAC EDUCATION GROUP COMPANY

Please visit our web site at: www.garethstevens.com
For a free color catalog describing Gareth Stevens Publishing's
list of high-quality books and multimedia programs,
call 1-800-542-2595 or fax your request to (414) 332-3567.

Library of Congress Cataloging-in-Publication Data

Gentle, Victor.
    Lynxes / by Victor Gentle and Janet Perry.
        p. cm. — (Big cats: an imagination library series)
    Includes bibliographical references and index.
    Summary: Describes the physical characteristics, behavior, and habitat of lynxes.
    ISBN 0-8368-3028-8 (lib. bdg.)
    1. Lynx—Juvenile literature. [1. Lynx.] I. Perry, Janet, 1960- II. Title.
    QL737.C23G485   2002
    599.75'3—dc21   2001049696

First published in 2002 by
Gareth Stevens Publishing
A World Almanac Education Group Company
330 West Olive Street, Suite 100
Milwaukee, WI 53212 USA

Text: Victor Gentle and Janet Perry
Page layout: Victor Gentle, Janet Perry, and Tammy Gruenewald
Cover design: Tammy Gruenewald
Series editor: Catherine Gardner
Picture Researcher: Diane Laska-Swanke

Photo credits: Cover, pp. 5, 11, 13, 17 © Alan & Sandy Carey; pp. 7, 9, 15, 19 (inset),
21 © Tom & Pat Leeson; p. 19 (main) © Steve McCutcheon/Visuals Unlimited

Printed in the United States of America

1 2 3 4 5 6 7 8 9 06 05 04 03 02

Front cover: Falling snow chills bare trees and earth, but this cool cat is warm and dry in its thick fur coat.

TABLE OF CONTENTS

Words that appear in the glossary are printed in **boldface** type the first time they occur in the text.

COOL CATS

Winters are cold and dark for half the year in Canada and the northern United States. This is where Canadian lynxes live. The Sun shines less. Days are shorter. Nights are chilly or icy cold.

Staying alive in the cold is no problem for cats that are built for it. Canadian lynxes have feet like snowshoes and lots of warm fur. With their super-sharp eyes, they see better at night than any other cats. They can hunt alone or together when they want to. Canadian lynxes are such cool cats they can take the cold.

Lynxes take care to stay hidden, or they sit very still. When these lynxes sit still, their frosty color is hard to see against a snowy background.

DRESSED TO LIVE

Canadian lynxes have short, thick fur. It keeps the cats warm and dry. Raindrops and snowflakes hardly ever make their skin wet. Lynxes lose little body heat to the icy winds.

Fur also helps lynxes hunt. As they run, their large, furry feet spread out and help them speed on top of the snow. **Prey** that have short, small feet punch holes in the snow's crust. Their bodies sink into deep, powdery snow, and they are easier for lynxes to catch.

A lynx strolls on top of the crusty snow. Look at the size of those paws! How long its legs are! The lynx seems to be all paws and legs!

WHERE AND BEWARE HAIR

Lynxes have **whiskers** around their eyes and mouths. These long, stiff hairs help them feel their way in tight spots.

Hair grows longer and in thick layers around the necks and faces of Canadian lynxes. These fancy fur collars, called **ruffs**, help keep lynxes warm. Ruffs make them look bigger, too. That may scare off wolves and other animals that want their food or their **territory**.

These **kittens** have grown ruffs and are getting big. It is almost time to leave their mother.

EXTRA SENSOR EYES

Like all cats, lynxes are **predators** and eat only meat. Predators hunt other animals. Super-strong eyesight helps cats be quick and sure when they hunt.

A cat's eyes see very well in dim light. Inside each eye is a kind of mirror, called the **tapetum lucidum**. The tapetum brightens any light a cat sees — just as you see more light when you put a shining light bulb in front of a mirror.

The **tapeta** in the eyes of a lynx are larger than the tapeta in the eyes of other cats. In the dark, lynxes see better than any other cats.

In a cat's eye, a black strip lets in light. The shape of this strip changes to let in more light at night — and less in bright sunlight.

HAIRY HEARING

A cat's ears are made for hearing soft sounds. The large, triangle-shaped parts of a cat's ears are called **pinnae**. Pinnae move around to catch sounds that our small ear flaps never hear. A cat can hear a mouse moving underground!

Lynxes have long hairs on the tips of their pinnae. These hairs pick up even more sound. Lynxes are the best night hunters of all cats, because they can hear and see better than other cats.

Mom and kitten rest in daytime. The kitten's blue eyes are nearly blind. In four weeks, its eyes will be brown and see as well as its mother's eyes.

HUNTING HARES

Canandian lynxes are very picky eaters! They would eat snowshoe hares at every meal, if they could. Why might that be?

For one, snowshoe hares are just the right size for catching and eating. A 2-pound (1-kilogram) hare is enough food for two days for one lynx. Secondly, lynxes mostly live and hunt alone. A snowshoe hare is the biggest prey that one lynx can handle easily.

Sometimes two lynxes might spot each other watching a deer — and suddenly they will set their sights higher.

A snowshoe hare zigzags to escape a lynx. If they have to, lynxes will hunt **voles**, birds, squirrels, beavers, and insects, instead.

LINKS TO THE LAND

Snowshoe hares are very important to lynxes. In years when there are few snowshoe hares, mother lynxes have only one or two kittens. In years when there are many snowshoe hares, the same lynxes have four or five kittens. More snowshoe hares in the forest means more lynxes, too!

Lynxes **mate** in late winter. In spring, their kittens are born. The kittens grow strong in the warm summer. Then, they can survive the cold winter.

These lynx kittens wait near their **den**. When they are ten months old, kittens leave their mothers. They then make their own territory and hunt alone.

GROWING, GROWING, GONE!

Lynx kittens grow fast. Before they are a year old, they leave their mothers. Grown lynxes must keep from fighting and getting hurt. They **mark** their territories, warning other lynxes to stay away.

Also, lynxes must steer clear of other predators, such as wolves, bears, and bobcats. The most dangerous predators for lynxes are humans. People kill lynxes for fur, and they move into the land lynxes need to live and hunt. People make it hard for lynxes to survive.

Hunters use dogs to chase lynxes into trees, where they are easy targets. Inset: A lynx marks its territory to keep animals away.

COOL AND CLEAN

Lynxes are part of the **balance of nature**. People from Europe brought snowshoe hares to North America so that they had food to hunt. Hares became the lynxes' favorite meal. If lynxes did not love to eat hares, there would be far too many hares.

Hunters often take heads from moose and deer as trophies, leaving the bodies behind. This "trash" makes an easy meal for hungry lynxes.

When humans leave messes in the forest, lynxes clean up. That's very cool. But lynxes *are* very cool cats!

These fine-looking lynx kittens wear their fur coats better than any human would — or should.

MORE TO READ AND VIEW

Books (Nonfiction)   *Big Cats* (series). Victor Gentle and Janet Perry (Gareth Stevens)
Cats. Animals Are Not Like Us (series). Graham Meadows
(Gareth Stevens)
Hunter in the Snow: the Lynx. Susan Bonners (Little, Brown)
Look Once, Look Again (series). David M. Schwartz (Gareth Stevens)
Mammals. Wonderful World of Animals (series). Beatrice MacLeod
(Gareth Stevens)
Wild Cats: Cougars, Bobcats, and Lynx. Deborah Hodge
(Kids Can Press)

Books (Activity)   *Prehistoric Mammals: A New World.* Melvin Berger (Putnam)

Books (Fiction)   *The Animal Family.* Randall Jarrell (HarperCollins)

Videos (Nonfiction)   *Cubs and Kittens and Other Wild Babies.* (Adventure Productions)
The Fascinating World of North American Predators. (Stoney Wolf)
North America. Wild about Animals (series). (Madacy Entertainment)

PLACES TO VISIT, WRITE, OR CALL

Lynxes live at the following zoos. Call or write to the zoos to find out about their lynxes and their plans to preserve lynxes in the wild. Better yet, go see the lynxes, person to cat!

The Montgomery Zoo
P.O. Box Zebra
Montgomery, AL 36109
(334) 240-4900

Northwest Trek Wildlife Park
11610 Trek Drive East
Eatonville, WA 98328
(360) 832-6117

Papanack Park Zoo
150 Nine Mile Road
Wendover, ON, Canada K0A 3K0
(613) 673-PARK

The Minnesota Zoo
13000 Zoo Boulevard
Apple Valley, MN 55124
1-800-366-7811

WEB SITES

Web sites change frequently, but we believe the following web sites are going to last. You also can use a good search engine, such as **Yahooligans!** [*www.yahooligans.com*] or **Google** [*www.google.com*], to find more information about lynxes, other big cats around the world, and their homes. Some keywords that will help you are: *lynxes, bobcats, North American wildlife, European lynxes,* and *snowshoe hares.*

www.yahooligans.com
Yahooligans! is a great research tool. It has a lot of information and plenty to do. Under Science and Nature, click on Animals and then click on The Big Picture: Animals. From there, you can try Animal Videos, Endangered Animals, Animal Bytes, BBC Animals, or Natural History Notebooks and search for information on lynxes, forests, mountains, and American wildlife.

www.leopardsetc.com/meet.html
Leopards, Etc. lets you hear big cats. Click on the speaker icon next to each cat name. You can hear all kinds of big cats roaring, growling, rasping, barking, and purring.

www.nationalgeographic.com/features/ 97/cats/
National Geographic has a really cool game that lets you design the perfect predator.

www.kidsplanet.org
On *Kids' Planet* by Defenders of Wildlife, you can play games and view the Web of Life story. You also can learn how to join other people in saving endangered wildlife.

www.nhm.org/cats/
The Natural History Museum of Los Angeles County has a really great exhibit called *Cats! Mild to Wild.* Click on Biology, and you will find how cats are built, how they use their claws, teeth, legs, and voices — and more!

www.epa.gov/students/ecosyste.htm
The *Environmental Protection Agency Student Center* is a great place to learn about the places that lynxes live, to see other endangered species and the places they live, and to find out what you can do to help protect wildlife and the Earth.

www.eparks.org/flash.html
The *National Parks Conservation Association* includes wildlife facts and information about national parks. Click on Wildlife Protection and then on Wildlife Facts. From there, choose Lynx to get facts, its endangered status, threats, and the national parks where it lives.

www.vrd.org/locator/subject.shtml#science
Do you have more questions about lynxes? Try *Ask an Expert.* This site has scientists and naturalists who will help you find out whatever you need to know.

GLOSSARY

You can find these words on the pages listed. Reading a word in a sentence helps you understand it even better.

balance of nature (BAL-uhns of NAY-chur) — the numbers of animals that would exist if humans did not interfere 20

den (DEN) — the place where animals give birth, hide their cubs, and sleep 16

kittens (KIT-uhns) — the babies of lynxes 8, 12, 16, 18, 20

mark (MARK) — leave a scent or scratches to warn other animals that a territory already belongs to a lynx 18

mate (MAYT) — come together to make babies 16

pinnae (PIN-ee) — triangle-shaped parts of a cat's ears — that is, the parts you see 12

predators (PRED-uh-turs) — animals that hunt other animals for food 10, 18

prey (PRAY) — animals that are hunted by other animals for food 6, 14

ruffs (RUHFS) — thick layers of long hair that look like collars around the necks of lynxes 8

tapetum lucidum (tuh-PEET-uhm LU-suhd-uhm) — mirrorlike part of a cat's eye that gives the cat more light to see with; plural: **tapeta** (tuh-PEET-uh) 10

territory (TER-uh-tor-ee) — area of land that an animal (or a group of animals) marks out as its hunting ground 8, 16, 18

voles (VOHLZ) — small, mouse-like animals that have dark fur and live underground 14

whiskers (WIS-kurs) — long, stiff hairs near the noses, cheeks, and eyes of cats 8

INDEX